AMBER

by Melissa Blackwell Burke

HOUGHTON MIFFLIN BOSTON

Would you like to take a peek at how something looked long, long ago? If so, just look at a piece of amber that has an insect in it. Amber looks like a clear, golden gem. How does an insect come to be part of a beautiful stone?

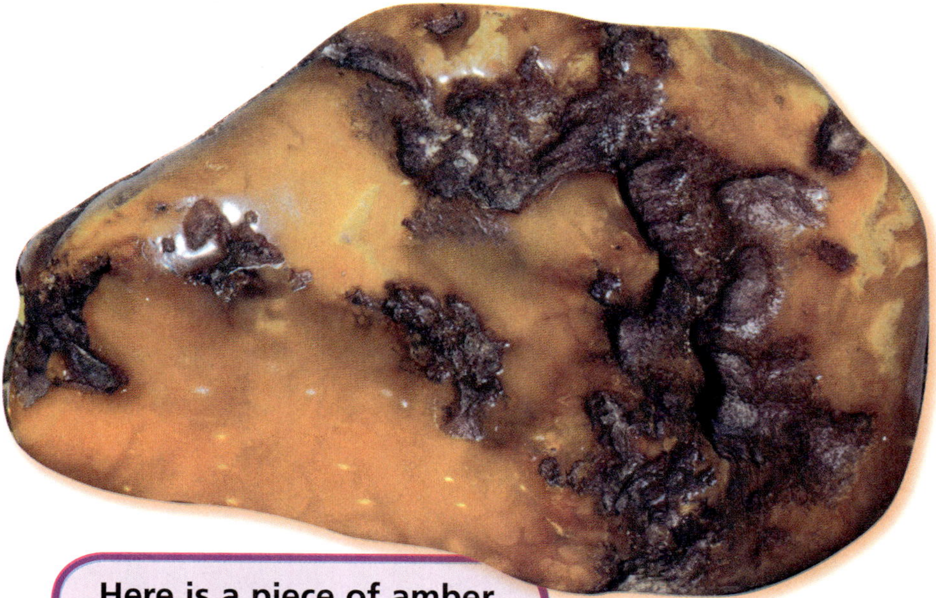

Here is a piece of amber before it is polished.

Millions of years ago, thick forests covered parts of Earth. Animals both large and small lived in the forests. Many kinds of plants grew there, too.

In the forests, resin dripped from some of the tree trunks. Resin is a thick, sticky liquid that some plants make.

When the resin first fell from the trees, it was soft and sticky. Sometimes leaves and flowers fell into the resin. They became stuck.

Some live insects got trapped in the soft resin, too. Most of the insects were small. Large insects were usually able to get out of the sticky resin.

These are some of the colors of amber.

Over a very long time, the resin changed. Heat and pressure helped turn the resin into hard lumps. These lumps of resin became a fossil called amber. Amber is mostly yellow, but it also can be orange, brown, or sometimes red.

You can still see the things that were trapped in the amber. Some of them are a lot like plants and animals that live today. Others are kinds of plants and animals that are extinct, which means that they no longer exist.

Some paleontologists study amber. Paleontologists are scientists who study fossils. They do tests to find out how old an amber fossil is. Then they look at the plants and animals trapped in the amber. When they know the age of the amber, they know when these plants and animals lived. The scientists can also see if they look like today's plants and animals.

How are these insects trapped in the amber like insects that live today?

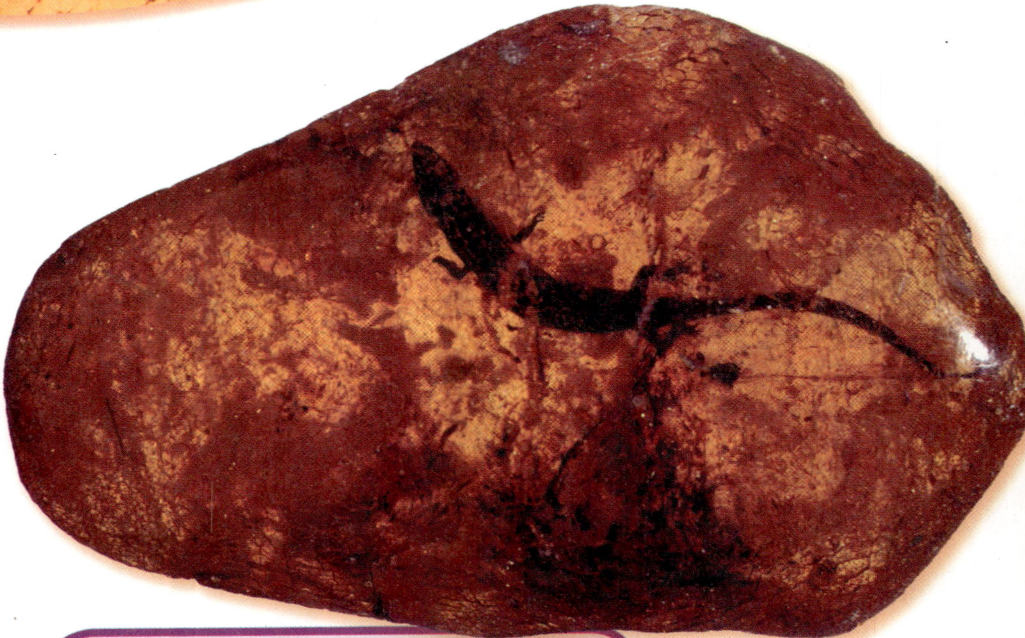

Sometimes even larger animals were trapped in amber.

People have found many, many amber fossils with insects in them. These include ants, flies, and mosquitoes. They also have found some amber with larger animals in it.

In a way, amber fossils give us a snapshot of the past. The leaves, flowers, and animals that were trapped in amber are almost frozen in time.